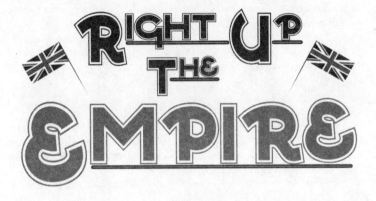

RIGHT UP THE EMPIRE

DIANE MASON & ANDREW SELWOOD

summersdale

RIGHT UP THE EMPIRE

Summersdale Publishers Ltd
46 West Street
Chichester
West Sussex
PO19 1RP
UK

www.summersdale.com

Printed and bound in Great Britain

ISBN: 978-1-84953-002-6

Substantial discounts on bulk quantities of Summersdale books are available to corporations, professional associations and other organisations. For details telephone Summersdale Publishers on (+44-1243-771107), fax (+44-1243-786300) or email (nicky@summersdale.com).

Acknowledgements

To the unsung illustrators of Victorian magazines and periodicals who *always* had enough lead in their pencils

Introduction

From the 1850s onwards, the explosion of the popular magazine market meant Victorians were provided with reading material covering all topics and catering for all tastes – nearly all of which was illustrated. From Mayfair to Manchester and beyond, any lady could get her visual fix of celebrities, beauty tips and the essentials of domestic life in *Woman at Home,* whilst the cosmopolitan man could feast upon *The Strand* for tales and pictures of adventure, heroism and soldiers of the British Empire subduing Johnny Foreigner.

Right Up the Empire sends up these images with brand new, raunchy captions to give you a sneaky glimpse of what the butler might have revealed had he been spying through the keyhole on the ladies and gentlemen of the time. Prepare to journey beneath the covered table legs of Victorian popular culture to uncover a hidden land of divas, dandy playboys, double standards, glamour and more sexual peccadilloes than you can crack a whip at.

It is with pride that we present an age where, secretly, morals were as loose as a dangling brassiere and absinthe made the heart grow fonder.

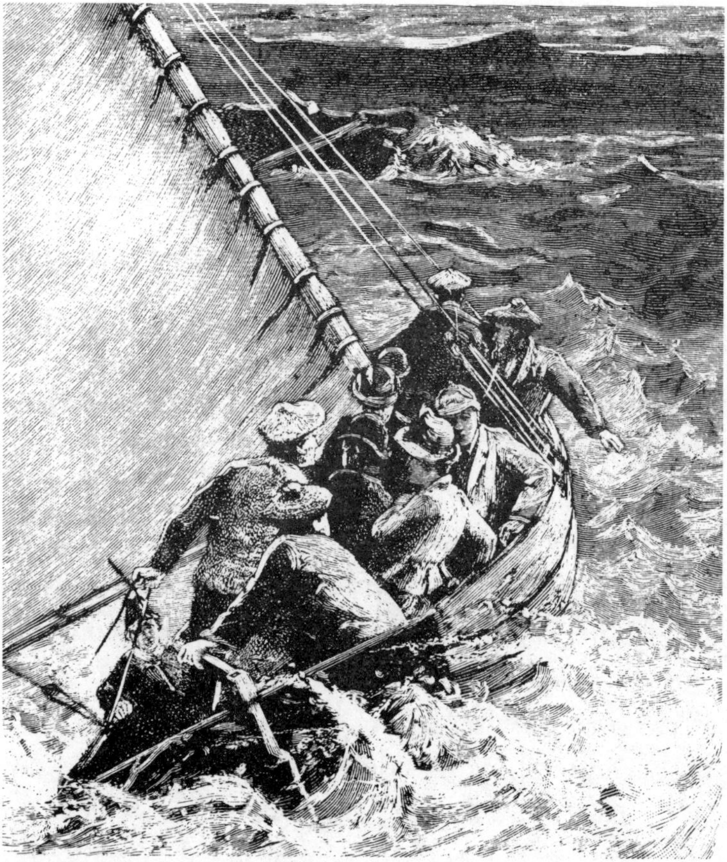

All was lost and a watery fate awaited everyone on board. In desperation, Jane turned to Simon and cried, 'Make me feel like a woman one last time!'

Not wishing to disappoint her, he ripped off his shirt and shouted, 'Iron this!'

'Oh,' sighed Alicia, 'the tea party was a disaster! The sandwiches were disgusting. I will not buy crab paste from that chemist again.'

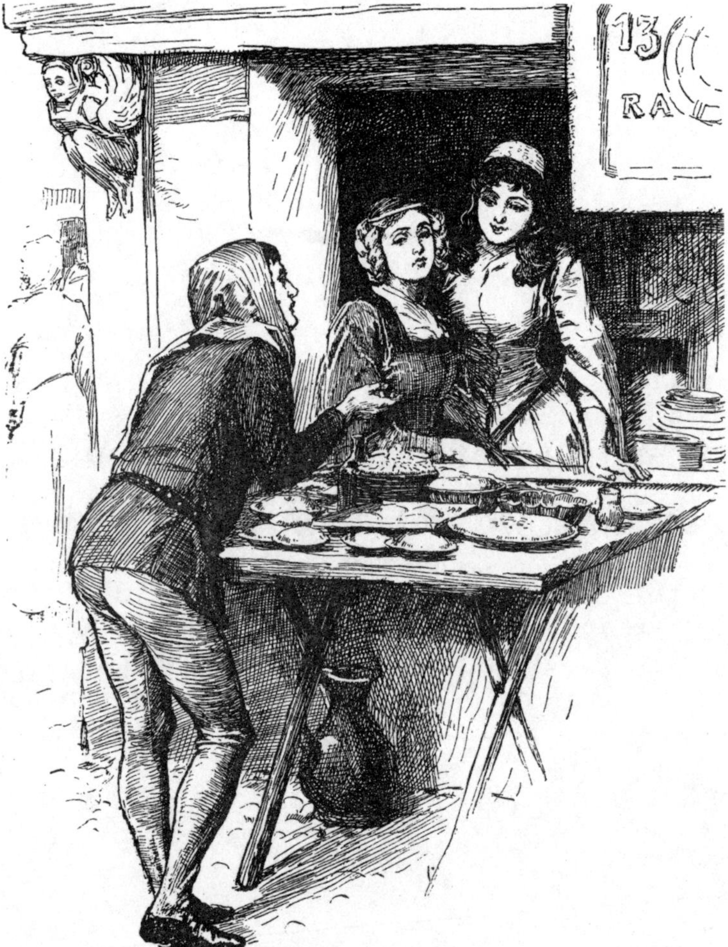
13
RA

Jack the Knave loved Madam
Ecstasy's Bakery – it was the only
place in town where you could grab a
pie and pick up a couple of tarts.

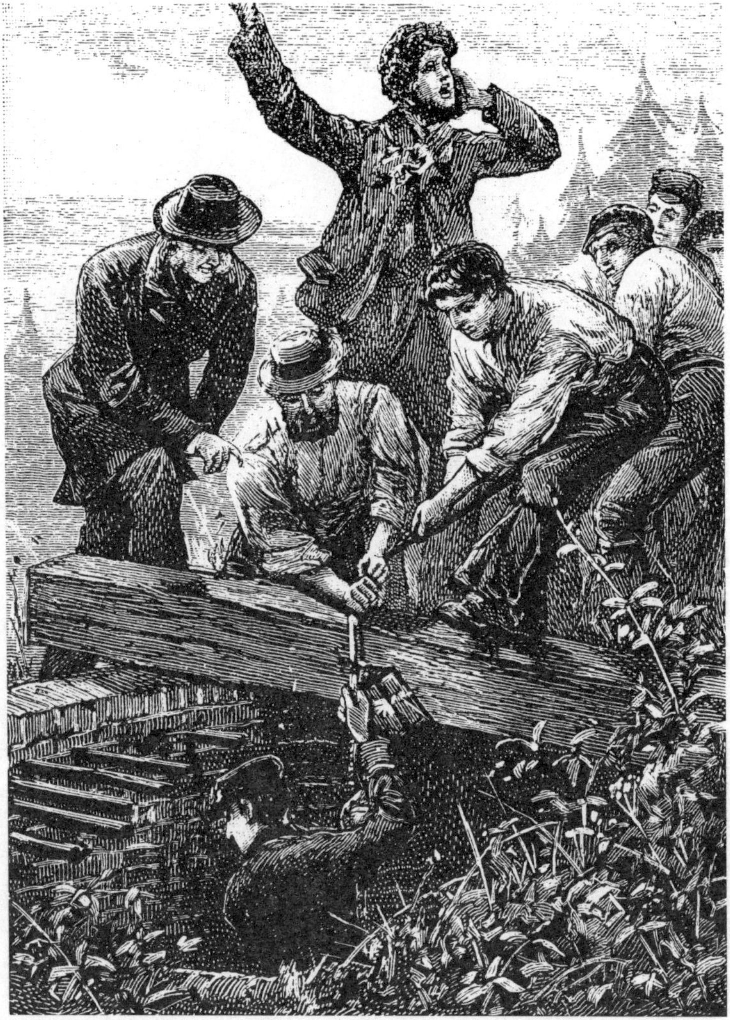

Though shy at first, Peregrine soon found a group of chums all eager to explore a manhole!

Professor Arbuthnot and his young wife, Matilda, eagerly planned their next palaeontological expedition. Colleagues agreed that she was an expert at digging up valuable old fossils.

After some initial language problems, Robinson Crusoe eventually explained to Man Friday how the division of labour was going to work.

Caroline, the milkmaid, was
devastated when the farmer's wife
gave her the sack because she
couldn't keep her calves together.

Midshipman Sheridan took the new recruit, Jack, on a trek up Brokeback Mountain and taught him how to blow the sailor's hornpipe.

Peter gave Elizabeth a mood ring. When she was in a good mood, it glowed green. When she was in a bad mood, it left a red mark on his cheek.

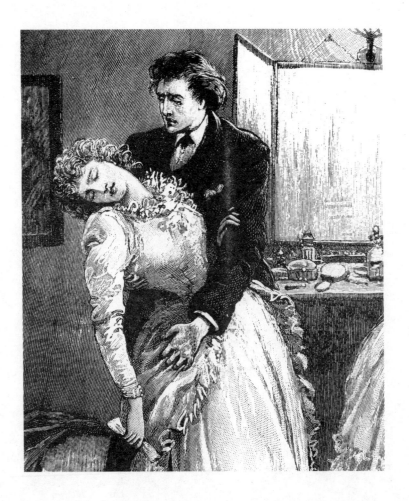

Young ladies swooned as soon as
Martin opened his mouth. Perhaps he
needed to overcome his fear
of the dentist.

Naturalists from miles around concealed themselves in the bushes to watch Flora pampering her tits at the window.

'Excuse me, is this the house of Zeno the Great, the world's most celebrated clairvoyant, who can see every aspect and detail of the future with perfect accuracy?'

'It is, sir.'

'Was he expecting me?'

Rudolph's wife was a sex object;
whenever he suggested
sex, she objected.

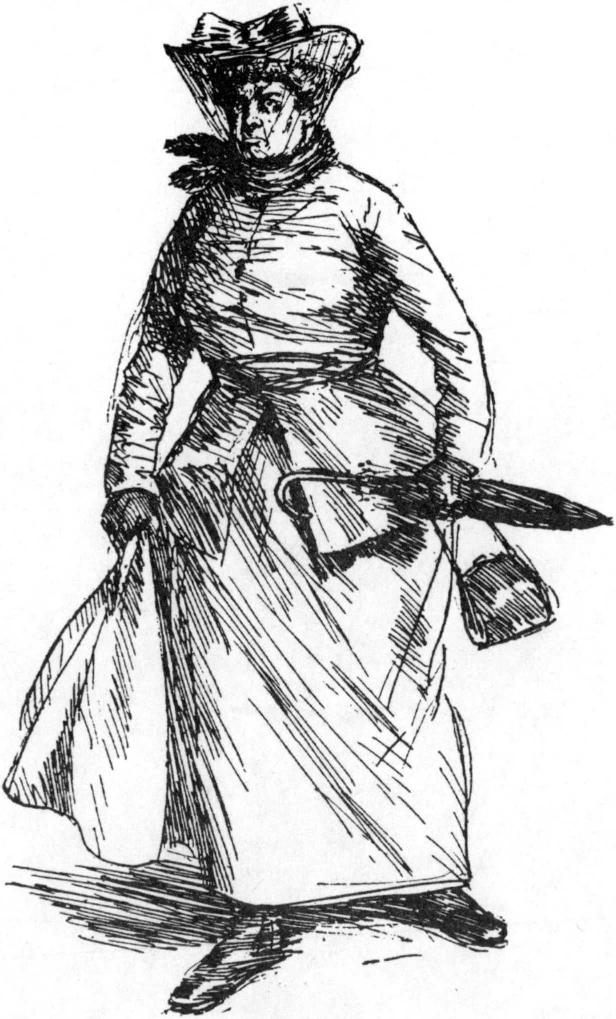

Bertram enjoyed his nights out at The
Transvestites Arms. It was the kind of
pub where he could eat, drink
and be Mary.

When the vicar's bike went missing, he decided to base his next sermon on the Ten Commandments and emphasise 'Thou Shalt Not Steal' to prick the conscience of the guilty party. Unfortunately, he had got as far as 'Thou Shalt Not Commit Adultery' when he remembered where he had left it.

‘How pissed was I last night?!’

No one liked to comment, but Julia's bum really did look big in that.

Old Edwina tried a mudpack to make herself more beautiful. It worked for a while, but then it dried up and fell off.

While recovering from an operation to remove a mole from the end of his penis, old Mr Potter vowed, 'I'll not try shagging one of those savage little varmints again!'

John's wife was an excellent housekeeper. When they divorced she kept both houses.

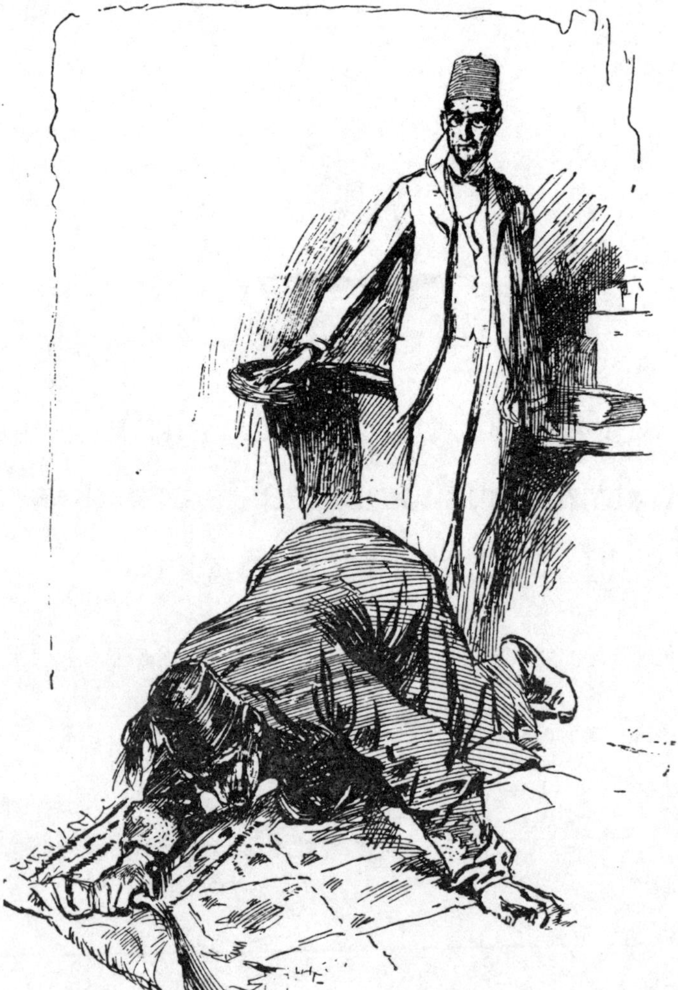

One of the Pasha's favourite
entertainments was watching Ali and
his performing tapeworm.

Mr Darcy discovered there was one thing his bank account and his sex life had in common: if you've got no money, you don't get much interest.

'If I took Viagra,' enquired Mr Williams, 'would I be able to get it over the counter?'

The pharmacist looked thoughtful and replied, 'Yes, if you took two tablets.'

Errol knew that he had married 'Miss Right'. But it was much later that he discovered her first name was 'Always'.

Last Christmas, the neighbours were agog when young Tom invited Mrs Jones to kiss his ass.

Happy couple Michelle and Cara were setting up home in the countryside. They sent for Bob, the carpenter's lad, to quote for some repairs to a door. Young Bob suggested a couple of joints and a good nailing, but Michelle and Cara explained that they preferred tongue and groove.

'Is there anything you have in common?' demanded the frustrated marriage guidance counsellor.

'Well,' replied Mr Smith, 'neither of us sucks cocks.'

It wasn't long before members of the Chislebury Hunt decided that the wholesale consumption of absinthe prior to the chase was not a good idea.

'I'd like to buy a parrot, please,'
said Gertrude.

'Have you had any experience?'
replied the assistant.

'I've had a cockatoo.'

'I don't doubt that, madam, but have
you kept birds before?'

Old Harry felt quite ill after the discovery of a grey pubic hair. It was in his kebab.

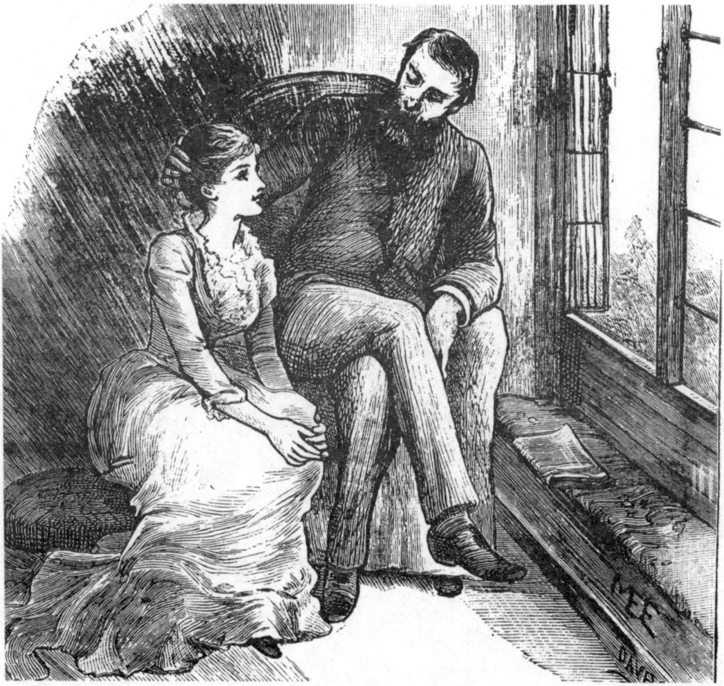
MEE

'Come, Ettie,' said Mr Conway the music teacher. 'It is time for you to get your lips around my horn!'

Dr Brain, the psychologist, said, 'Tell me, what does this ink blot look like?'

Old Mr Edwards turned a ghostly white and replied, 'It's a blob of pure evil, sucking the souls of men into a vortex of misery and damnation!'

'Oh, I do beg your pardon,' replied Dr Brain. 'That's a picture of my wife.'

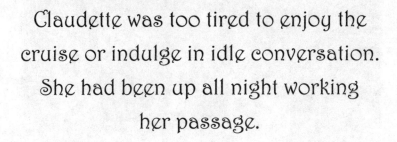

Claudette was too tired to enjoy the cruise or indulge in idle conversation. She had been up all night working her passage.

Ruben was vulgar and uncouth. He thought nothing of handling Jemima's jugs in the marketplace.

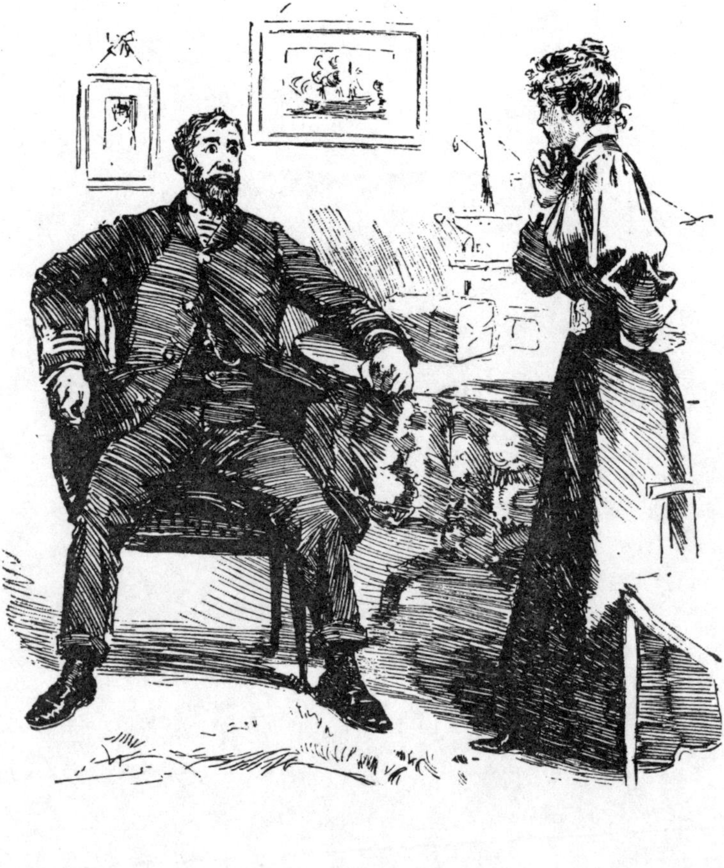

Mr Bartlett took antihistamine with his Viagra so when he got an erection it wasn't to be sneezed at.

Jane loved her climbing expeditions.
She even helped to carry the ropes,
and rumour had it amongst the guides
that she could take a good length.

Sally got an antique gold pocket watch from her husband on his death bed. For a dying man, he put up quite a fight.

There was a dilemma at Barney's Backyard Zoo. The female gorilla was ready to mate but the males were not interested. In desperation, Barney asked Wilf, the cage cleaner, if he would have sex with the gorilla for £20.

Wilf said, 'Yes, but can you give me a fortnight to come up with the £20?'

'Come upstairs and take off all my clothes!' demanded Daisy. She was sick of living with a transvestite.

When Dan was interviewed for his job at the blacksmith's forge he was asked if he had any experience shoeing horses. Dan replied, 'No, but I once told a donkey to fuck off!'

Jane was rather a plain girl but she enjoyed the company of military men. She wasn't so keen on the cavalry, though, because they often charged.

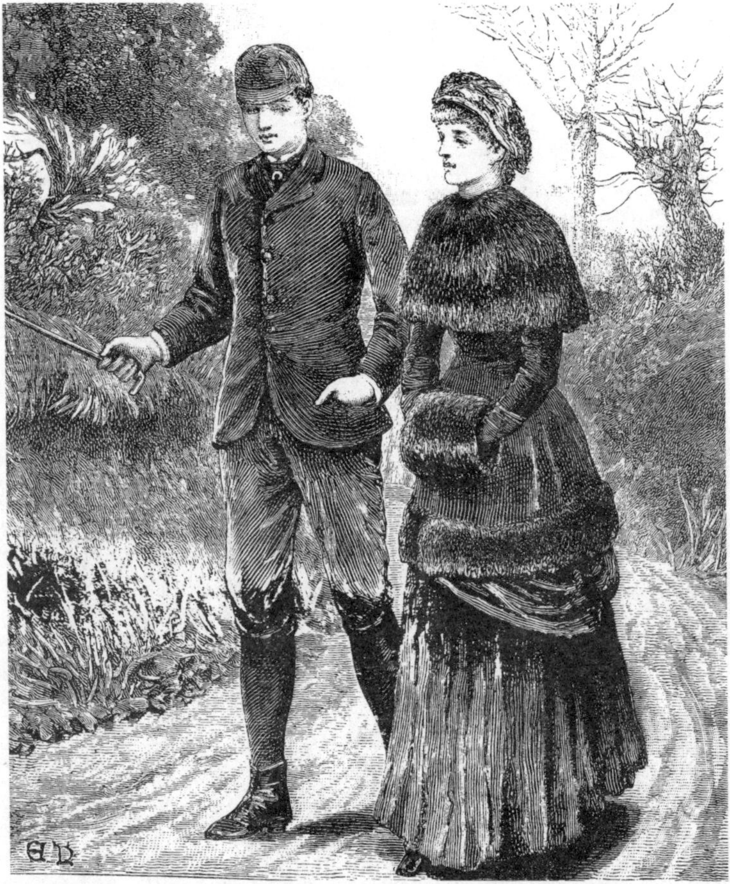

Sir Peter was astounded when he discovered that it was possible to get both hands into Esther's muff.

Martha discussed her desires with Mr Arkwright, the builder. He was a popular character, renowned for his dependable erections.

A couple of locals told Smeethson
that he could get pussy down the
Delhi Road. As he has been missing
for a fortnight, we assume that
he found some.

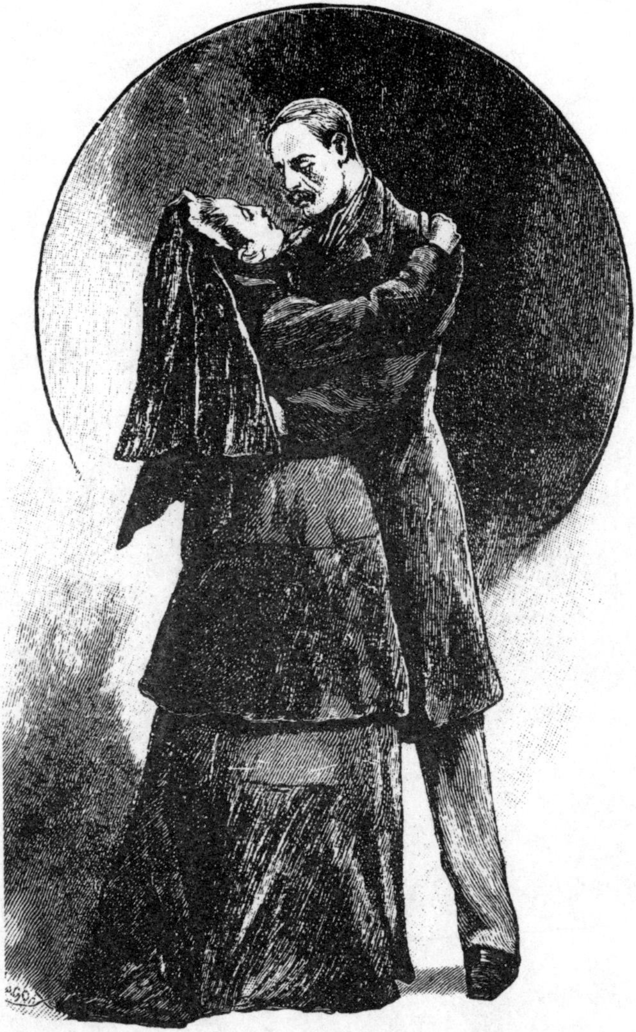

After much research, John, a
dedicated naturalist, recently decided
that the difference between a fox and
a walrus is about seven pints.

All sorts of trouble erupted when Sir Cyril misunderstood the charitable act of holding a policeman's ball.

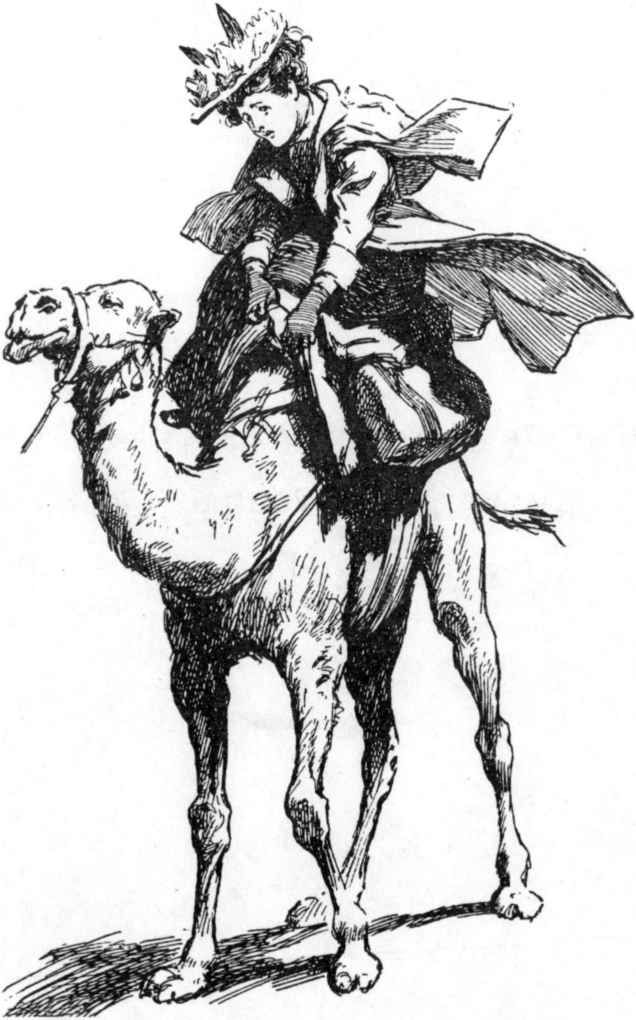

When in Egypt, Gillian disliked riding
horses. She always preferred
a good hump.

Nicholas was overwhelmed when
Karen wore her bingo dress.
'Eyes down, look in.'

'Is that new perfume I smell?'
asked Malcolm.

Antoinette replied, 'It is – and you do!'

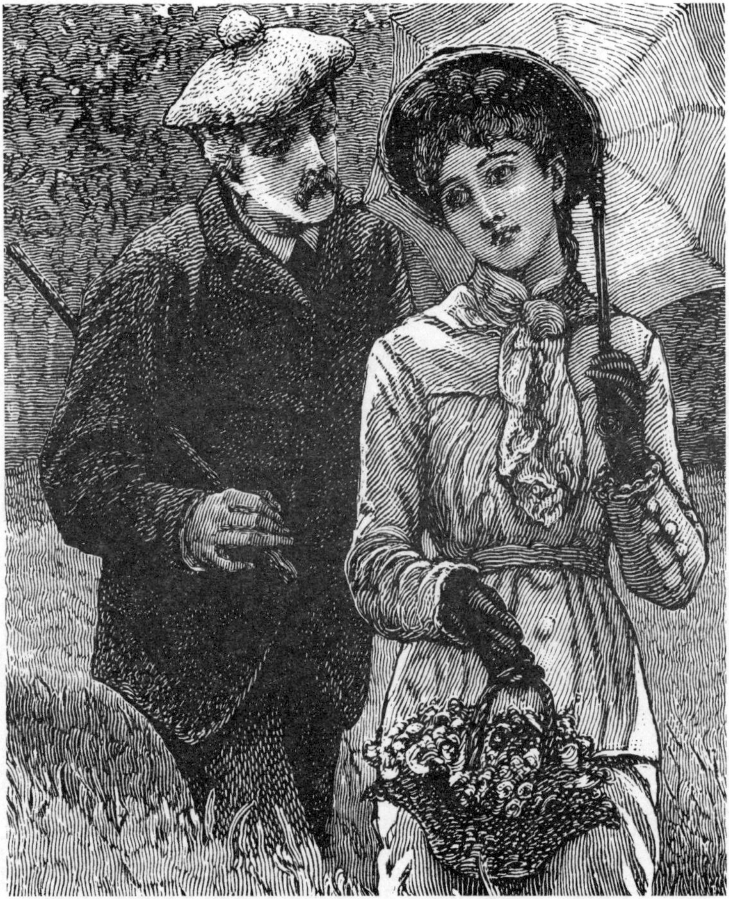

As a keen gardener, Esmeralda couldn't wait for Gordon to explore her bloomers.

A goose in the rushes, flat on her
back, was typical of that hussy Emily!

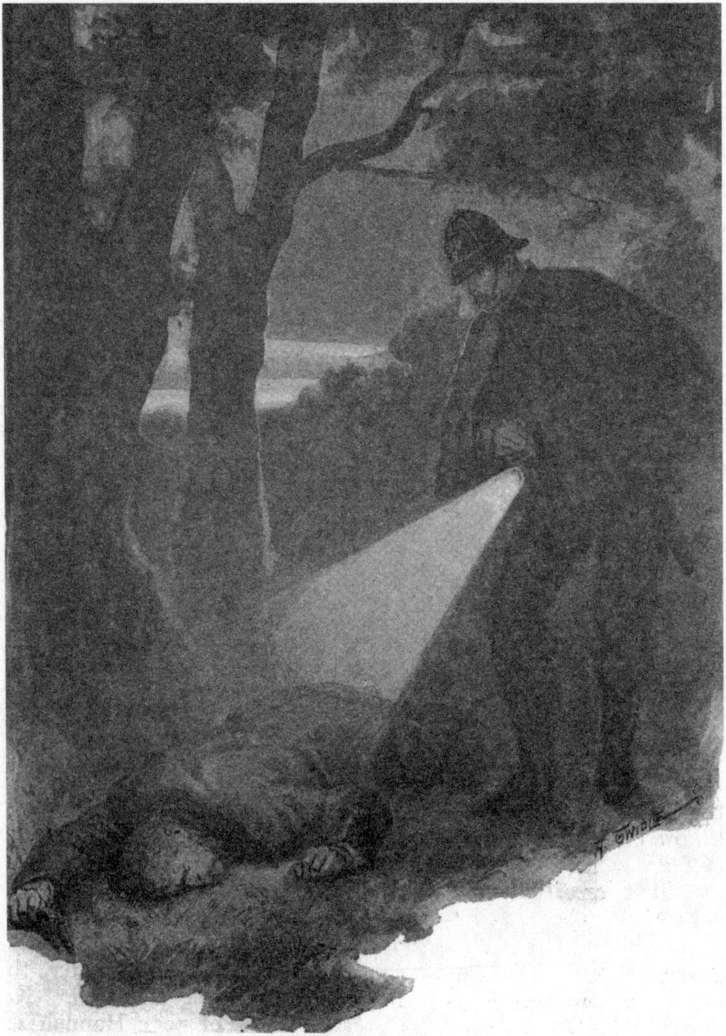

PC Tarquin was not at all shocked by the discovery of a man's body. He was no stranger to handling a stiff one in the woods.

'So I said to her,' explained Dr Smedley, the anatomist, 'you have two hundred and six bones in your body – now let's make that two hundred and seven!'

Jim had a reputation as a hard man
on the rugby field. He would always
make sure his opponents
felt his tackle.

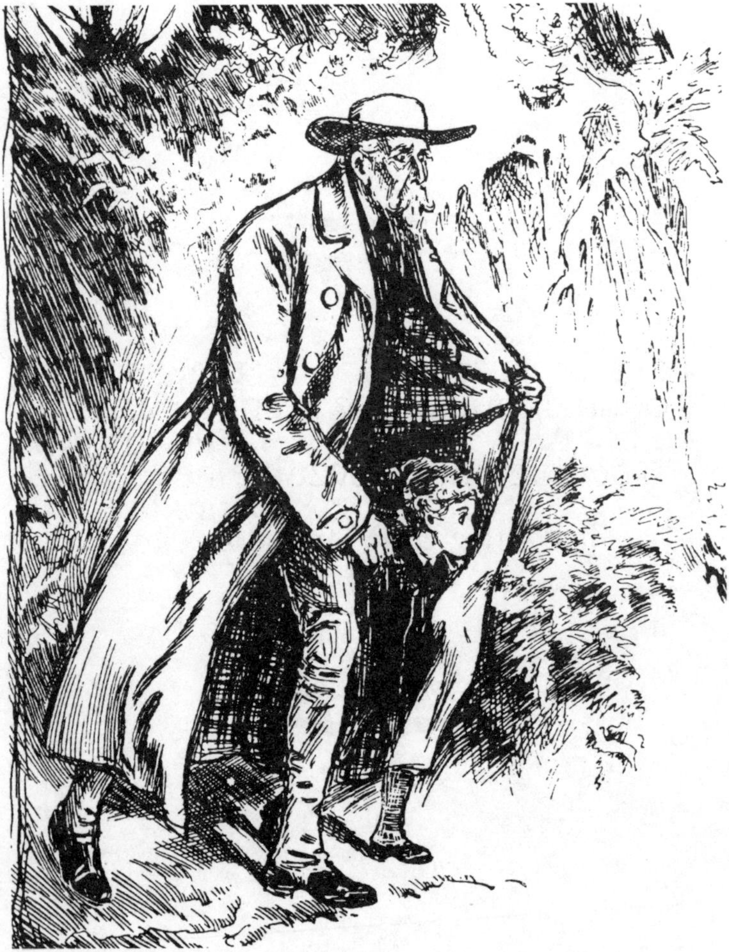

Today, Ignatius the inept entertainer accidentally revealed how the 'Jake-the-Peg' trick worked.

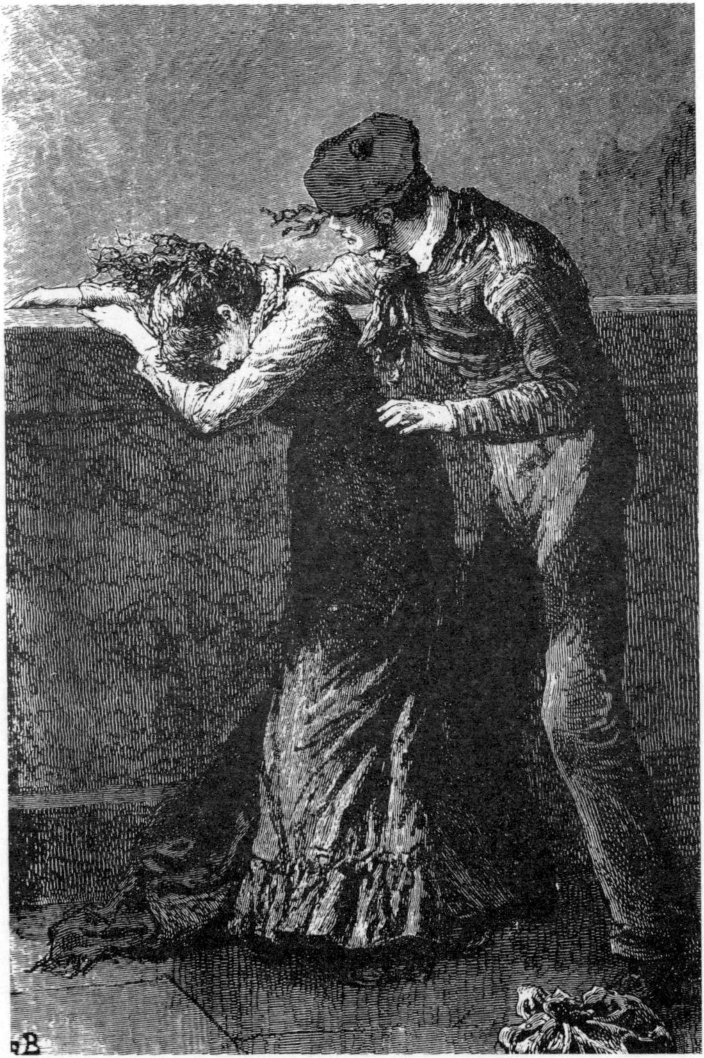

She was the admiral's daughter,
so she was used to dealing with
discharged seamen around
the naval base.

'I say, my good man, can you direct
me to the Westbury turn-off?'

'Oh yassur, she works down there in
the post office!'

Isabella found an ideal way to make a fruit cordial. She complimented him on his choice of shoes.

Joy was rather like a lava lamp: fun to look at but not too bright!

Cleo was determined to ride side-saddle despite Brendan's attempts to persuade her to try a leg-over.

'Tell me, General,' said Herbert, 'If the Turks invade the rear, would Greece help?'

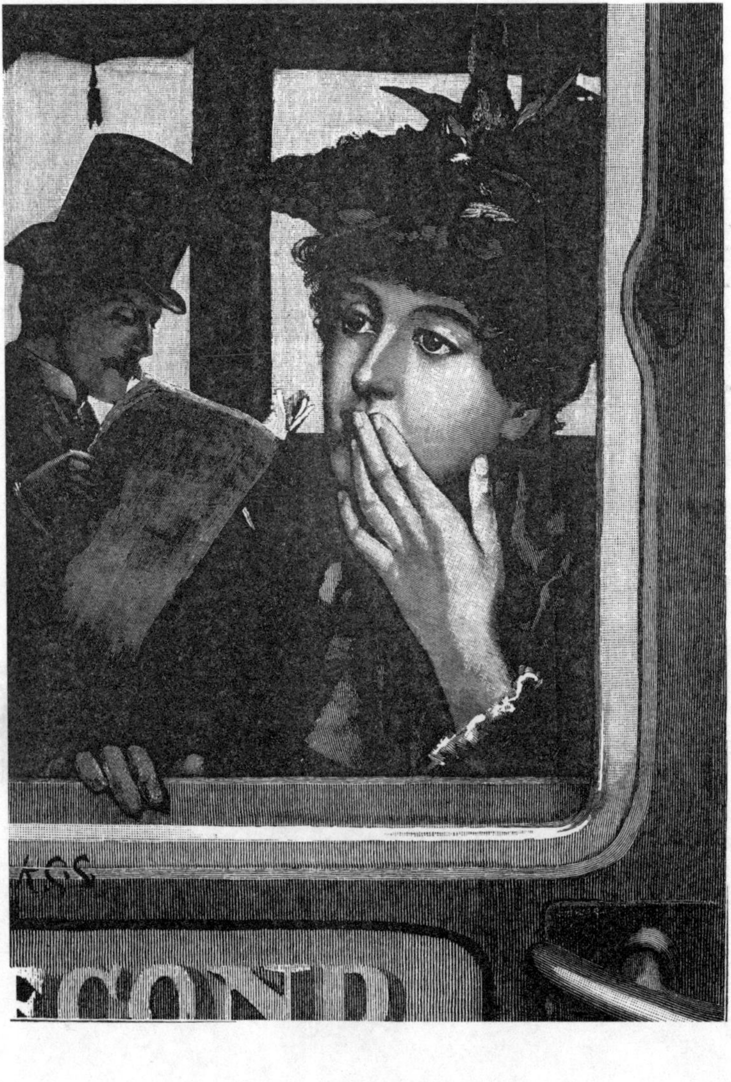
COND

When the 12.15 from Paddington broke down, the driver struggled in vain for some 35 minutes to repair the engine without any tools. Eventually a lady leaned out of the carriage window and said, 'I think you need a screwdriver.'

He replied, 'If you're offering, madam – it'll be ages before the engineer gets here!'

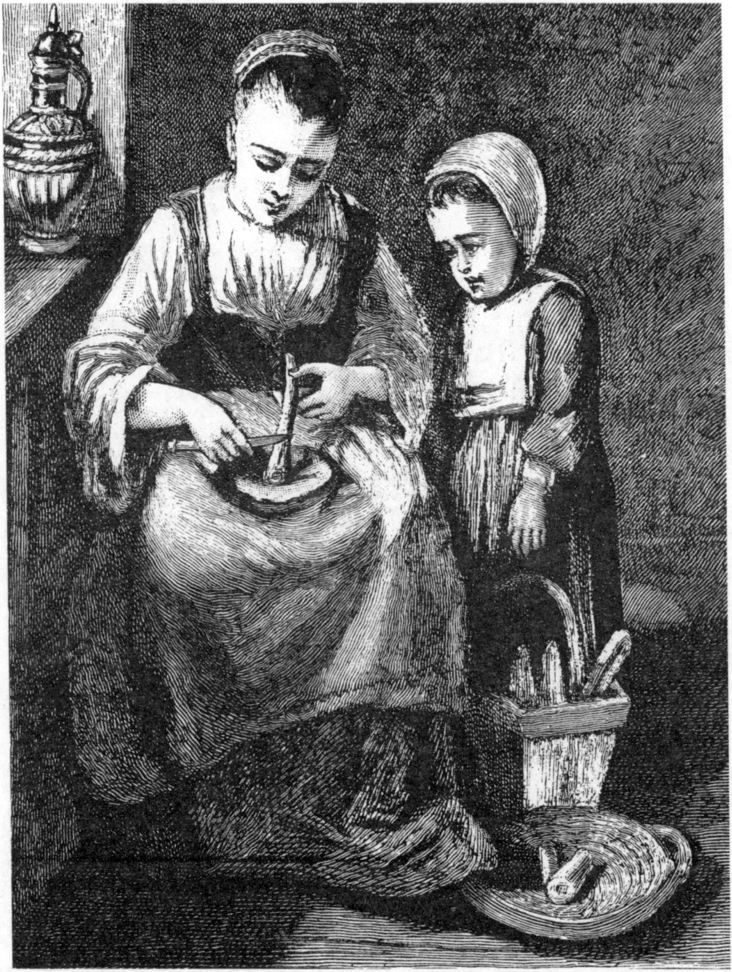

'What's that, mother?'

'It's a little something to keep me company, darling, when your father goes away travelling.'

'Here's that sick squid I owe you.'

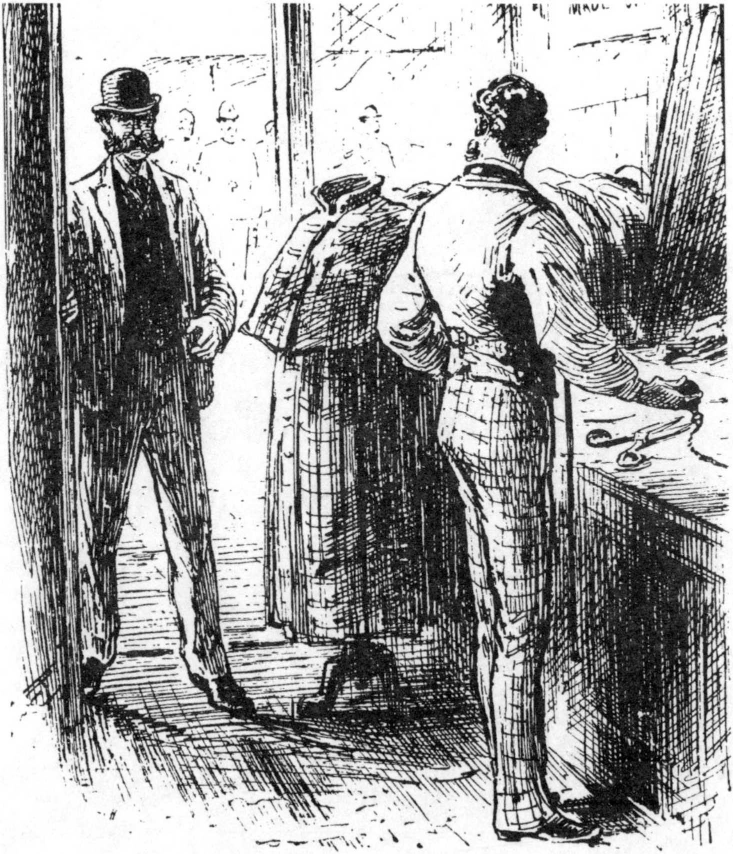

'Good morning, old chap, I think I
need some spectacles.'

'I think you're right, sir – this
is a tailor.'

Kate helped retired Major Phipps along the platform. He had had problems walking unaided ever since his days in the Lancers, when he was kicked by a horse in the Dardanelles.

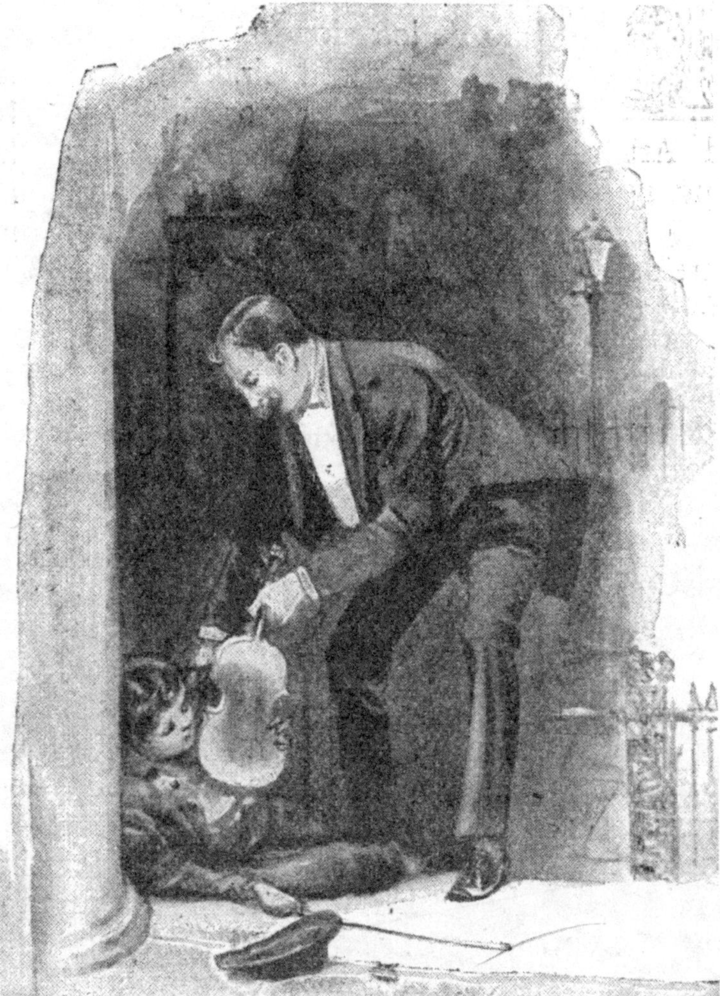

Algernon was convinced that he was afflicted with tinnitus until he beat the busker to death.

After losing his job at the embassy in
Algiers, Jerome was often
strapped for cash.

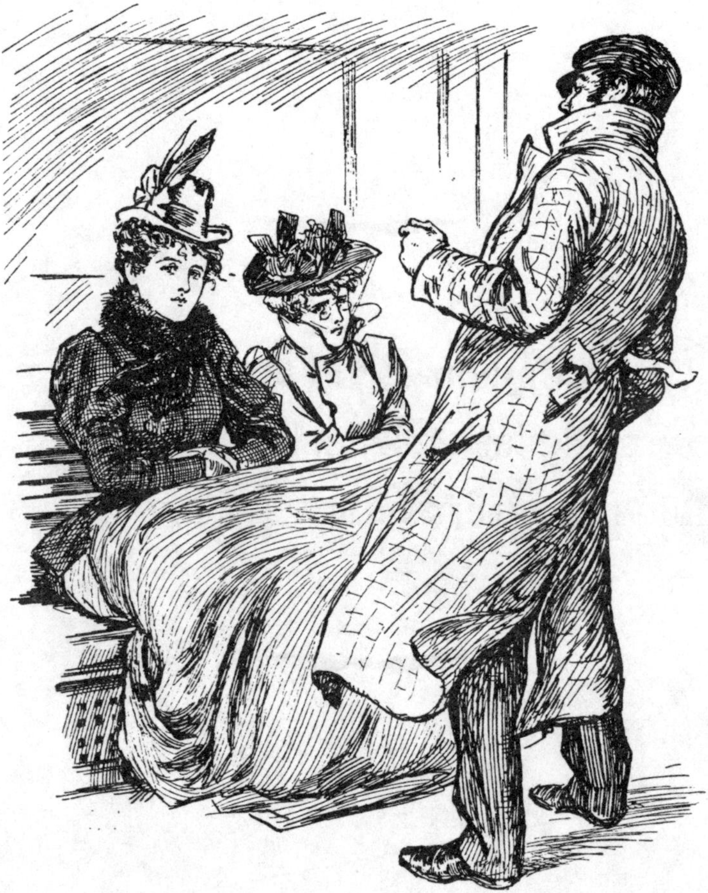

The two plain-clothes lady officers
arrested Jack the flasher and he was
duly tried for handling swollen goods.

From a prone position, Charles could
get a much better view of
Clara's pussy.

'My wife has a twin,' said Gerald.

'Goodness!' replied Samantha, 'How
do you tell them apart?'

'Her brother has a beard.'

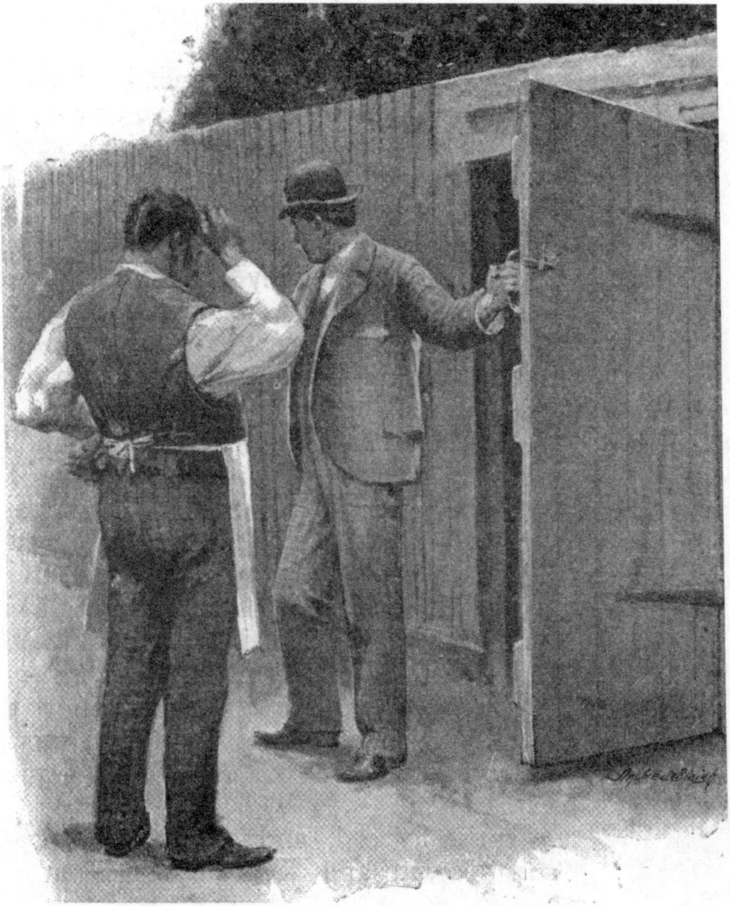

Tristan always checked that the coast was clear before inviting his chums to use the tradesman's entrance.

Blind Old Ron never did find out why it was that all his friends found his young granddaughter so repulsive.

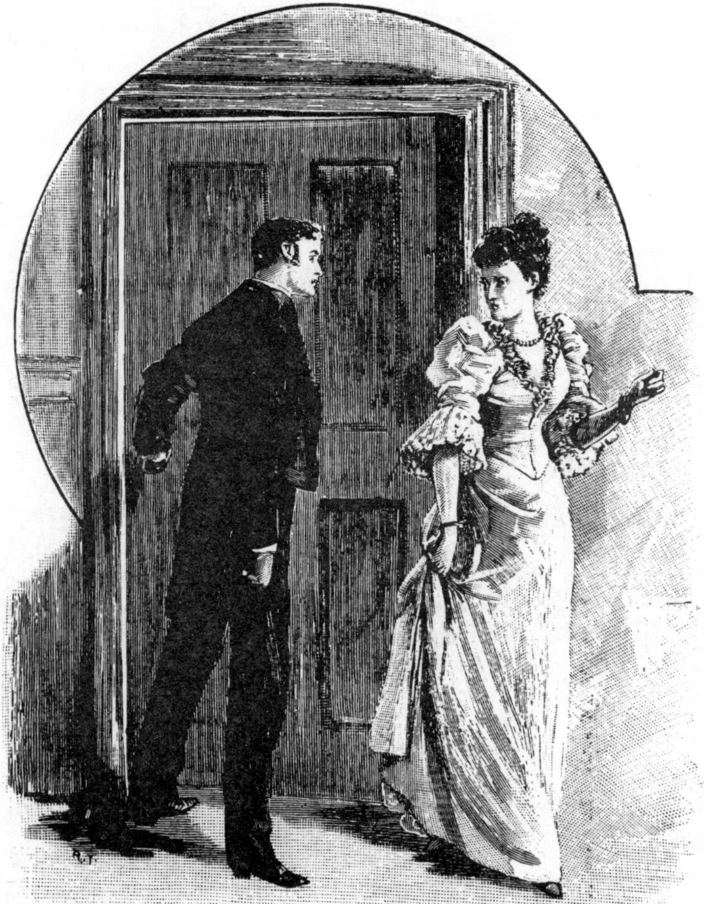

Helena, the high-class hooker, said, 'I will perform any service for ten pounds.'

Gervaise looked thoughtful for a moment and replied, 'Paint my house.'

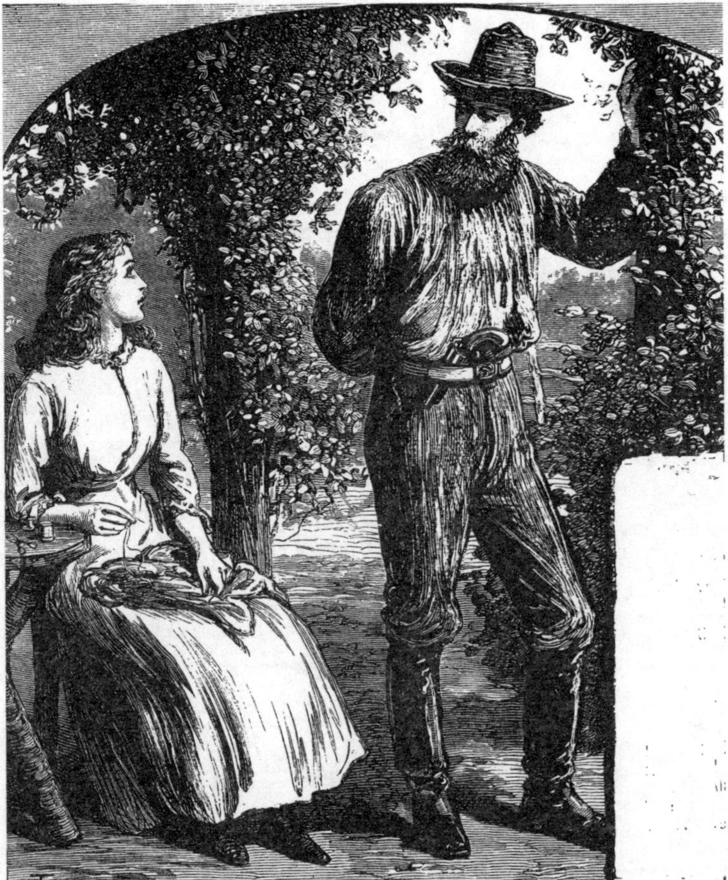

Trapper Jake may only have had one arm, but Flossie knew that he was still an expert at getting beaver.

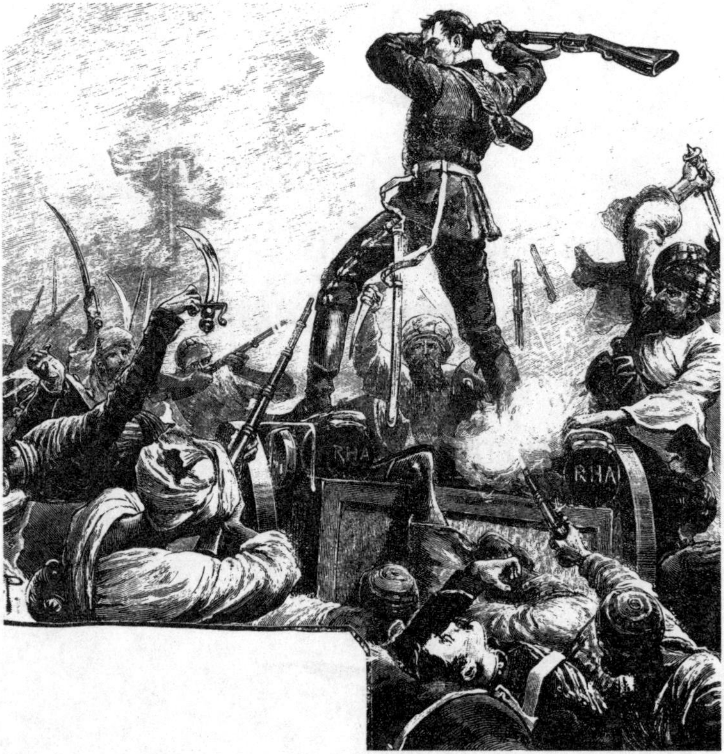
RHA
RHA

Every cloud has a silver lining. The battle was lost and Captain James sustained a bullet wound to the groin. But he returned to Cambridge certain of a place in the Coxless Four.

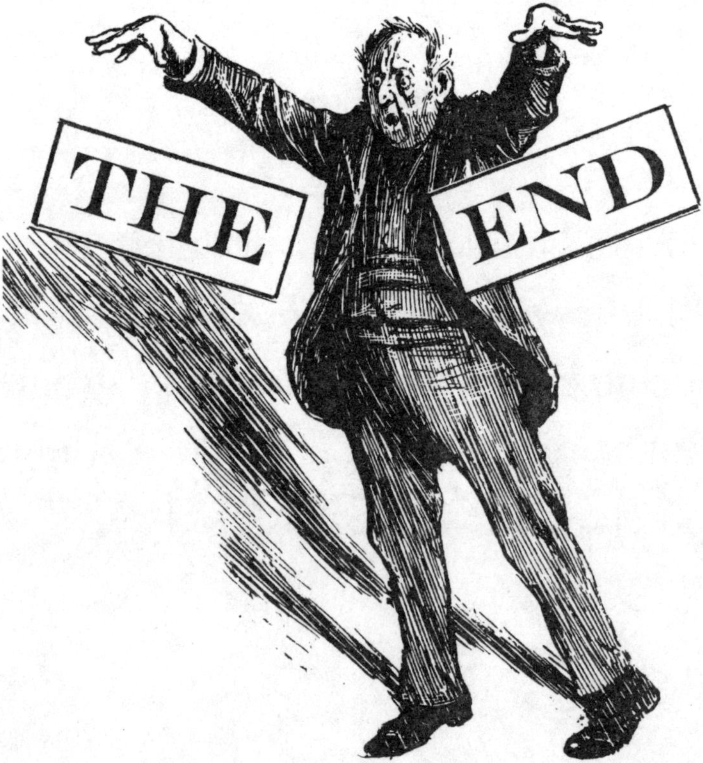
THE
END

Have you enjoyed this book? If so, why not write a review on your favourite website?

Thanks very much for buying this Summersdale book.

www.summersdale.com